www.gardenpublishingco.com

Spirit of Holiness

The Garden Training Center, Inc.
An Apostolic School of Ministry

Copyright ©2022 by The Garden Training Center, Inc.
Published by Garden Publishing Company LLC
For more information, please visit gardenpublishingco.com

All rights reserved. No parts of this publication may be reproduced, stored in a retrieval system, or transmitted in any form or by any means, electronic, mechanical, photocopying, recording, or otherwise, without the prior written permission of the copyright owner.

This book is sold subject to the condition that it shall not, by way of trade or otherwise, be lent, resold, hired out, or otherwise circulated without the publisher's prior consent in any form of binding or cover other than that in which it is published and without a similar condition including this condition being imposed on the subsequent purchaser. Under no circumstances may any part of this book be photocopied for resale.

Scripture taken from the New King James Version of the Bible ©. Used by Permission, all rights reserved.

ISBN 978-1-7355464-8-3
Cover design by Garden Publishing Co./BTSM
Interior design by Garden Publishing Co.

Printed in the United States of America.

Acknowledgments

Holy Spirit is the inspiration for the content of this book, however someone put words to it. This book was written by Danetta Ferguson.

This book is one of a series of books written and distributed by The Apostolic School of Ministry from The Garden Training Center, Inc. The series arises from the foundational teachings of the school of ministry, founded by Brandy Helton. Brandy wrote several sections that are included in each book such as "God's Love" and the prayers included at the end of each book.

Many thanks to the team of writers of the series for their collaboration to make the series available to the public. The writers are: Lauren Caldwell, Jessica Doggett, Danetta Ferguson, Paula Green, Elisa Griffith, Nancy Hadley, Robin Harmon, Brandy Helton, Grant Hill, and Kevin McSpadden. Each have sought Holy Spirit for the words He wants to speak through them. The result is a mixture of personalities and communication strategies that convey the total message in a beautiful, diverse way.

A special thanks goes to Nancy Hadley, Kevin Mc-

Spadden and Chelsey Butcher with Garden Publishing Co., for their preparation and fine tuning of the text.

Encouragement and Prayer for the Reader

Beloved of God, these teachings are written to reveal Jesus Christ and His heart of love for all who call upon His name to save them.

God has sent His only begotten Son, Jesus Christ, to save all who would believe in Him and His Word.

God desires to reveal Himself and to give us His divine nature in Christ Jesus our Lord through the power of His Holy Spirit.

God is Jealous. He wants us to encounter His presence daily and walk with Him in glory – intimate communion - today, while it is called today, and forever.

It is my prayer that this teaching would so impact the readers that all would come to know and believe JESUS, the King of Kings and Lord of Lords, our Great God and Savior, and receive the PERFECT LOVE He has for us all as we grow up into Him and mature as true sons and daughters of God.

May you grow in faith and knowledge of your God and Savior and come to know the love that He has for you. I pray for you the Apostle Paul's prayer for spiritual growth:

Ephesians 3:14-21 The Living Bible (TLB)
"14-15 When I think of the wisdom and scope of his plan, I fall down on my knees and pray to the Father of all the great family of God—some of them already in heaven and some down here on earth— 16 that out of his glorious, unlimited resources he will give you the mighty inner strengthening of his Holy Spirit. 17 And I pray that Christ will be more and more at home in your hearts, living within you as you trust in him. May your roots go down deep into the soil of God's marvelous love; 18-19 and may you be able to feel and understand, as all God's children should, how long, how wide, how deep, and how high his love really is; and to experience this love for yourselves, though it is so great that you will never see the end of it or fully know or understand it. And so at last you will be filled up with God himself.
20 Now glory be to God, who by his mighty power at work within us is able to do far more than we would ever dare to ask or even dream of—infinitely beyond our highest prayers, desires, thoughts, or hopes. 21 May he be given glory forever and ever through endless ages because of his master plan of salvation for the Church through Jesus Christ."

In Christ our Lord,
Brandy Helton
A child of God

God's Love

God's love is good news! Don't believe the lie that God is distant, unapproachable, and angry!

God is love. He is the only true, eternal God. He is perfect and holy, and He is truth. God is One. He has revealed Himself in three distinct, individual, equal persons: God the Father, God the Son – Jesus, and God the Holy Spirit.

The Bible tells the story of God's perfect love. In that love, God created the first family to live on the earth with Him. Through their deep intimate relationship with the Father, Adam and Eve were meant to fulfill all that was in God's heart on Earth just like it is in Heaven, for God's glory and purposes. Adam and Eve were chosen to walk with God, clothed in His glory presence and were perfect, as He is perfect, and they lived in His beautiful garden, the secret place called Eden. He gave them His breath, life and power to have dominion over all He created and wanted them to reproduce that LIFE replenishing the earth with it, until all the earth is filled with His glory.

Genesis 1:26-28
"26 Then God said, 'Let Us make man in Our

image, according to Our likeness; let them have dominion over the fish of the sea, over the birds of the air, and over the cattle, over all the earth and over every creeping thing that creeps on the earth.' 27 So God created man in His own image; in the image of God He created him; male and female He created them. 28 Then God blessed them, and God said to them, 'Be fruitful and multiply; fill the earth and subdue it; have dominion over the fish of the sea, over the birds of the air, and over every living thing that moves on the earth.'"

God created His children in His likeness. He made them spirit beings, with a soul – mind, will and emotions – and placed them in a physical body. He gave His children the choice to love Him and to walk with Him in obedience to His every word. He gave the first family the power to overcome any temptation offered to them through God's adversary, the devil, who had rebelled against the Most High God in Heaven's glory and was cast down to the earth. The devil, Satan, brought great darkness and chaos prior to Adam and Eve's existence.

Adam and Eve were deceived into thinking that God was not perfect in love as Satan, the adversary, tempted them to believe that God would not keep His Word to them. Through their own will, Adam and Eve disobeyed the Father by eating from a tree that had the power to open their eyes to both good and evil. Through their choice of disobedience, they willfully gave their inheritance and authority over to the devil and his kingdom. Sin entered mankind, which produced death, eternal separation from a Holy God. Adam and Eve were banished from the dwelling and intimacy of perfection in the garden and were sent into the world as a fallen creation.

Father God knew He had to come Himself and save His family, and in His wisdom, He chose to send His Son, Jesus Christ into the world to save us and restore fallen mankind back to relationship with Him. Through His Son, He destroyed all the works of the devil and the curse of death. Hebrews 9:22 says, *"And according to the law almost all things are purified with blood, and without shedding of blood there is no remission."* Remission means to cancel the penalty, so according to the law there must be shedding of blood to cancel the penalty for sin. The Father cancelled the penalty for the sins of His children through the shedding of the blood of His innocent, holy Son Jesus, who was the Sent One, called and chosen to die for all, so all could live.

John 3:16-21
"16 For God so loved the world that He gave His only begotten Son, that whoever believes in Him should not perish but have everlasting life. 17 For God did not send His Son into the world to condemn the world, but that the world through Him might be saved. 18 'He who believes in Him is not condemned; but he who does not believe is condemned already, because he has not believed in the name of the only begotten Son of God. 19 And this is the condemnation, that the light has come into the world, and men loved darkness rather than light, because their deeds were evil. 20 For everyone practicing evil hates the light and does not come to the light, lest his deeds should be exposed. 21 But he who does the truth comes to the light, that his deeds may

> *be clearly seen, that they have been done in God.'"*

Jesus was conceived by God's Holy Spirit in the womb of a young virgin named Mary. He appeared as the second Adam, in the flesh, with the choice to walk in perfect love and obedience, full of God's Spirit, as a man to do the will of His Father.

Jesus grew up as any male child did in the flesh but He had divine fellowship with His Father and Holy Spirit. At the appointed time, He was revealed as being sent from God to save. Jesus went around doing good and healed all who were oppressed by the devil spiritually and physically. He revealed His Father's heart and perfect love to all who believed through His teachings, grace and miraculous power.

Salvation means eternal life, healing, deliverance, protection, peace, wholeness, and forgiveness. Salvation came to all men through the cross, where the Son of God, the perfect One, was slaughtered as a lamb, bearing all sin for all times from a fallen people. Jesus bore the wrath of God against the darkness that separated God's family from Him. Jesus was punished for our sin and died to cleanse us from the guilt, shame and condemnation sin produces. Sin separates. Love restores.

Jesus was crucified, dead and buried, spending three days and nights in the depths of Hades, the realm of the dead fallen race. Jesus took back the keys of death and hell from that old serpent the devil, Satan, and therefore, all authority was restored back to Jesus.

Great Holy Spirit breathed LIFE into Jesus and raised Him from the dead. He appeared to His disciples, those who followed Him and obeyed His teachings. He showed them that He conquered sin, death and the grave and now, had the keys of hell and death, and would give ETERNAL LIFE to ALL who chose to believe in Him. King Jesus ascended back to the Father of glory where He ever lives to make intercession for us all, and He is coming again to the earth in power to establish His Father's Kingdom on Earth.

Jesus Christ is the head and Lord over His church, those who have made Him Lord and Savior, by believing He is the Son of the Living God and God in the flesh, who finished the work the Father gave Him to do. He not only died for our sins to save and heal us, He chose to give His authority to those He called and chose to follow Him as His disciples, His family.

Jesus has commissioned His followers to do the same works that He did while He lived on the earth.

John 14:12-14
"12 Most assuredly, I say to you, he who believes in Me, the works that I do he will do also; and greater works than these he will do, because I go to My Father. 13 And whatever you ask in My name, that I will do, that the Father may be glorified in the Son. 14 If you ask anything in My name, I will do it."

God loves us and desires that none should perish. He desires for His family to be with Him where He is. These books are written to inspire all who read them and to reveal the heart of God the Father, Jesus Christ the Son, and Holy Spirit in order that we might RECEIVE THE LOVE HE HAS FOR US and be CHANGED INTO HIS VERY LIKENESS. God desires to dwell with His family forever and ever just as He did in the beginning. How glorious it is to live in His presence and dominion, beholding His goodness, forever and ever, amen.

The book of Revelation describes the time that is coming when all things are made new according to God's heart of love:

Revelation 21:1-7
"1 Now I saw a new heaven and a new earth, for the first heaven and the first earth had passed away. Also, there was no more sea. 2 Then I, John, saw the holy city, New Jerusalem, coming down out of heaven from God, prepared as a bride adorned for her husband. 3 And I heard a loud voice from heaven saying, 'Behold, the tabernacle of God is with men, and He will dwell with them, and they shall be His people. God Himself will be with them and be their God. 4 And God will wipe away every tear from their eyes; there shall be no more death, nor sorrow, nor crying. There shall be no more pain, for the former things have passed away.' 5 Then He who sat on the throne said, 'Behold, I make all things new.' And He said to me, 'Write, for these words are true and faithful.' 6 And He said to me, 'It is done! I am the Alpha and the Omega, the Beginning and the End. I will give of the fountain of the water of life freely to him who thirsts. 7 He who overcomes shall inherit all things, and I will be his God and he shall be

My son.'"

To understand what is presented in the Bible, you must start by understanding God's love. The good news is that God loves you!

The Heart of It

God deeply desires for His people to reflect His holy nature. Unfortunately, for many people, a distorted understanding of true holiness leads to misperceptions of the nature of God, which prevents them from living a life that mirrors His glory. This book cuts right through to the very heart of holiness – the Spirit of Holiness working in believers to rid them of all that hinders them so that they can shine the light of God. It is a refining process, which may involve fire, but the end result is a holiness that is both pure and far more valuable than gold. Read on to learn about the holiness of God and the work of Holy Spirit to reproduce that holiness in your life.

Spirit of Holiness

The Word of God teaches us all throughout scripture of the Godhead: Father, Son, and Holy Spirit. They are often referred to as "the three in one," which reveals their perfect union. However, there is a distinct order within the Godhead. John 5:19 reveals, *"Then Jesus answered and said to them, "Most assuredly, I say to you, the Son can do nothing of Himself, but what He sees the Father do; for whatever He does, the Son also does in like manner."* It is obvious from this passage that Jesus is fully surrendered and under the direct authority of the Father in Heaven. This submission was part of what empowered Jesus to reveal the Father to the world. The Holy Spirit is also part of this empowering relationship.

Jesus speaks of Holy Spirit in John 16:5-15:
"But now I go away to Him who sent Me, and none of you asks Me, 'Where are you going?' But because I have said these things to you, sorrow has filled your heart. Nevertheless I tell you the truth. It is to your advantage that I go away; for if I do not go away, the Helper will not come to you; but if I depart, I will send Him to you. And when He has come, He will convict the world of sin, and of righteousness, and of judg-

> *ment: of sin because they do not believe in Me; of righteousness, because I go to My Father and you see Me no more; of judgment, because the ruler of this world is judged. I still have many things to say to you, but you cannot bear them no. However, when He, the Spirit of truth, has come, He will guide you into all truth; for He will not speak of His own authority, but whatever He hears He will speak; and He will tell you things to come. He will glorify Me, for He will take of what is Mine and declare it to you. All things the Father has are Mine. Therefore I said that He will take of Mine and declare it to you."*

The Helper spoken of in this passage is the Holy Spirit. He is the Spirit of Holiness, and He was sent by Jesus and draws from all that belongs to Jesus in order to give to us. Just as Jesus didn't do anything unless He saw the Father do it first, so the Holy Spirit always follows the direction of Jesus. He does nothing of His own initiative. It is important to understand than He is not a lesser part of the Trinity - He is not less important than the Father or the Son. He is an equal part of the Godhead, but each is subjected to and submitted to the proper authority. As with all things God does, this submitted relationship is based on love, and it serves to reveal God's righteous ways. But how does that apply to us?

When Jesus departed from the earth and ascended into Heaven, He sent us the Holy Spirit. When we receive Jesus Christ into our hearts as Lord and Savior by faith, Holy Spirit comes to dwell with us in our very being. Upon His arrival into our hearts, He promises never to leave us, fail us, or forsake us (Hebrews 13:5). Again, Holy Spirit is the Spirit of Holiness, so that reveals that each believer is empowered, just as Jesus was, to live a life of holiness before God.

The Bible has much to say about holiness. In fact, Hebrews 12:14 says, *"Follow peace with all men, and holiness, without which no one will see the Lord."* The New Living Translation (NLT) says it like this: *"Work at living in peace with everyone, and work at living a holy life, for those who are not holy will not see the Lord."*

We are given more instruction regarding holiness in 1 Peter 1:13-16.

> *"13 So prepare your minds for action and exercise self-control. Put all your hope in the gracious salvation that will come to you when Jesus Christ is revealed to the world, 14 So, you must live as God's obedient children. Don't slip back into your old ways of living to satisfy your own desires. You didn't know any better then. 15 But now you must be holy in everything you do, just as God who chose you is holy. 16 For the Scriptures say, 'You must be holy because I am holy.'"* (NLT)

Nobody knows us better than we know ourselves. Each of us knows our own weaknesses and our shortcomings better than anyone else does. Many times reading a scripture like this makes walking with the Lord seem like an impossibility. Our minds turn to thoughts such as, "I am far from holy. There's no hope for someone like me to walk with the Lord if holiness is what it takes." At one time or another, we have all had those mindsets. In order to break through some of these thought patterns, let's begin by gaining more understanding of holiness and the Spirit who leads us into it.

Speaking of Jesus, Romans 1:4 says, *"who was declared the Son of God with power by the resurrection from the dead, according to the spirit of holiness, Jesus Christ our Lord."*

When Jesus died and was placed in a tomb for three days, it was the power of the Spirit of Holiness that raised Him from the dead. Romans 8:11 tells us that *"if the Spirit of Him who raised Jesus from the dead dwells in you, He who raised Christ from the dead will also give life to your mortal bodies through His Spirit who dwells in you."* WOW! What a promise for you and me!

When we receive Christ by faith and Holy Spirit comes to dwell in us, our spirit man, having been dead, is restored to life and perfection. We can fully believe that we are made perfect in our spirit man because the Spirit of Holiness has made His home there. In that area of our being, there is nothing missing and nothing broken. All things have been made alive and brand new!

However, we still have some things to work out in the soul area of our makeup. The soul area consists of our minds, our wills, and our emotions, and as we walk with the Lord in the new journey we are on, the Spirit of Holiness resurrects, or brings to life, those places in us that are dead. Again, the *same spirit that raised Jesus from the dead* now lives in us and will perfect all that pertains to us. He will also bring to light anything that is unholy in us, and He will give us grace to overcome it.

It is very comforting to know that we don't have to become holy in our own strength. The truth is, we can't. Scripture says that apart from Christ we can do nothing, but through Him we can do all things. One of the most reassuring scriptures in the Bible is found in Philippians 1:6. It says, "*...being confident of this very thing, that He who has begun a good work in you will complete it until the day of Jesus Christ.*" If you are born again, it is because He has chosen you and He has willingly begun a work in you that He promises to bring to completion. Our job as believers is to fully submit to the Spirit of Holiness just as Jesus submits to the Father and the Spirit submits to Jesus. Working through our submission, it is the Spirit's job to make us holy. Take a deep breath and rest in that promise as we journey on through this book.

What is Holiness?

Scripture makes it very clear that God is a holy God. Revelation 4:8 says, "*Holy, holy, holy, Lord God Almighty, Who was and is and is to come!*"

Holiness is spoken of all throughout both the old and New Testament. From the Old Testament we learn that God's very nature is holy. Holiness refers to **the essential nature of God** and to **the very foundation of His being**.

"*The Lord is holy!*" Psalm 99:9

It doesn't get much clearer or simpler than that! Holiness is more than just a part of His personality. No, it is who He is!

The Old Testament also speaks of holiness as a **divine sacredness**. There were actual, physical places that were deemed holy in scripture, such as the location referred to in Exodus 3:5. Moses is told, *"Do not draw near this place. Take your sandals off your feet, for the place where you stand is holy ground."*

Holiness can also be described as **wonder, awe, dread and majesty**. In Genesis 28:17 we read, *"How awesome is God in this place! This is none other than the house of God, and this is the gate of heaven."*

Have you ever been in the presence of someone famous? Perhaps at a concert with a popular band, or a seminar with a well-known motivational speaker? The excitement and awe of the crowd for these people literally changes the atmosphere in the room. How much more when we have revelation of the God of heaven being in our midst? When He is present, the entire place, wherever that may be, becomes holy ground. It is exciting to realize that because the Spirit of Holiness has come to dwell in our hearts, the place where He dwells in us has become holy ground, too. Your body is the temple of the Holy Spirit. That's why we can say that our spirit man is pure and holy.

Very similar to the description of wonder, awe and dread is **worship, trembling and reverence**. We see this in Psalm 96:9. *"Worship the Lord in holy array; tremble before Him, all the earth."* When the Bible speaks of trembling in worship, it is not speaking of being afraid of God, but it does mean that we recognize, honor, and respect the fact that we are in the very presence of the Almighty

God, the Creator of the universe. To say that He deserves our respect is quite an understatement. There really are no words to describe the honor He deserves, but to speak of trembling gives us a very good picture. He is HOLY, and in His presence, we are on HOLY GROUND!

In Hosea 11:9, God proclaims, "*I am God and no man, the Holy One in your midst.*" There is a **separateness and a deity** in holiness. God is not to be identified with anything in creation. The very nature of God is total apartness from all that is common, unclean, profane, or evil. I've heard it stated that many times, even as believers, we spend a lifetime trying to create God in our image instead of allowing God to perfect us into His. Numbers 23:19 confirms this by saying, "*God is not a man, that He should lie, nor a son of man, that He should repent.*" He is separate and apart from anything and everything. There truly is none like Him in all the earth!

The Old Testament also describes holiness as **righteousness and purity**. Isaiah 5:16 says, "*But God who is holy shall be hallowed in righteousness.*" Habakkuk 1:13 refers to purity stating, "*You are of purer eyes than to behold evil, and cannot look on wickedness.*"

Having established throughout the Old Testament the holiness of God, the New Testament affirms that message, but it also speaks directly to believers to encourage us that the Spirit of Holiness is working in, with, and through us, bringing us into the very image and likeness of our Father. This great miracle of '*C*hrist *is us, the hope of glory*' (Colossians 1:27) is only available because of the cross and the sacrifice that Jesus made for us there.

The Old Testament spoke of the Day of Atonement and how that was a holy time for the inner cleansing of sin through the blood of the animal's sacrifice. The animal's blood was shed once a year in the Day of Atonement to cleanse the people of their sins before the Lord. When Jesus chose to give up His life to die on a cross, He became our Sacrificial Lamb. His shed blood covered our sin once and for all. No longer did the shedding of blood have to be repeated year after year. Because of this sacrifice, the Spirit of the Living God can now reside in us, since we have been washed in that precious blood. There is immeasurable power in the blood of Jesus – enough power to purify us and make us holy, spirit, soul, and body, if we are only willing to fully submit to that power.

As we read earlier, **God's people are called to holiness**, according to 1 Peter 1:16. We are to be holy because He is holy, and He is living in us. Ephesians 1:4 tells us that *"He chose us in Him before the foundation of the world, that we should be holy and without blame before Him in love."* There is so much rich truth in that scripture: 1) You and I are chosen by the God of the universe. 2) He chose us before the foundation of the earth...before time began! 3) We are chosen to be holy and without blame. 4) All of this is because of His great love for us.

As we discussed in the first pages of this book, nobody knows us like we know ourselves, and from earth's perspective that is a true statement. However, there is One Who knows us better than we know ourselves, and that One is our Father in Heaven. When He chose us before the foundation of the earth, He knew every word we would ever speak, every thought we would ever have and every sin we would ever commit...and He chose us anyway! Why? Because He loved us and He wanted a family. Furthermore, He is completely confident that the Spirit of Holiness will move mightily in us so that our lives and all that concern us will be perfected.

As believers, **we are declared holy and righteous through faith in Jesus Christ**. Hebrews 10:10 tells us that "*We have been made holy through the sacrifice of the body of Jesus Christ.*" This verse says that we 'have been' made holy. That is past tense, meaning it is already done. When Jesus declared the words from the cross, "It is finished", He meant it. Everything that needed to be done for you and me to be made holy was complete! We are now called "saints" - holy ones - all because the Spirit of Holiness dwells within us.

The work of the cross is now fully complete, but we are still a work in progress. Holy Spirit is working with us daily to rid us of things that are no longer fitting for a child of God. He is also giving us revelation of who He is and who we are so that we can grow into the vessel He created us to be. 1 Thessalonians 5:23 says, "*May the God of peace Himself sanctify you [that is, make you holy] entirely...spirit, soul, and body.*" Holiness is not only an internal reality for the believer, but also that which is to be perfected externally. 2 Corinthians 7:1 tells us, "*Let us cleanse ourselves from all defilement of flesh and spirit, perfecting holiness in the fear of God.*"

Believers, the saints of God, are deemed by Him to be "*a chosen race, a royal priesthood, a holy nation*" (1 Peter 2:9). God works though all of this so "*that He might present her to Himself a glorious church, not having spot or wrinkle or any such thing, but that she should be holy and without blemish*" (Ephesians 5:27). Beloved, the Father wants a bride for His son, and we, the church, are that bride. We are being prepared by the Spirit of Holiness for our wedding day!

As believers we live victoriously through the Holy Spirit. Our spirits are holy! May you really receive and encounter the reality that God's very presence lives within you. May you see and recognize that His Holy Spirit is changing you and taking you from glory to glory.

<u>All Things are Seen with God</u>

As we continue to discuss God's holiness and what it means for believers, it is important to recognize that literally nothing is hidden from God. Look at what these Scriptures reveal about God's all-seeing nature:

Hebrews 4:12-13
"*For the word of God is living and active and sharper than any two-edged sword, and piercing as far as the division of soul and spirit, of both joints and marrow, and able to judge the thoughts and intents of the heart. And there is no creature hidden from his sight, but all things are open and laid bare to the eyes of Him with whom we have to do.*"

Revelation 4:5-6

"5 And from the throne proceeded lightnings, thundering, and voices. Seven lamps of fire were burning before the throne, which are the seven Spirits of God. 6 Before the throne there was a sea of glass, like crystal. And in the midst of the throne, and around the throne, were four living creatures full of eyes in front and back."

God has many names in scripture. One of those names is El Roi, meaning "God Sees." The scriptures above clearly demonstrate that He sees all. We are all naked and laid bare before Him, and nothing is hidden from His sight. Because everything in and around us is laid bare before Him, the Spirit of Holiness is a master surgeon, dividing soul and spirit, removing those things that are poison and hurting us, and putting into us all that the Father created us to be. He doesn't just 'see' when we submit to Him. God sees everything and has seen it all from before the beginning of time! Nothing we've ever done has been hidden from His sight. We can't hide from God's presence and we can't fool Him. Once we realize that He already knows everything and still loves us immensely, submission to the lovingkindness of the Father should be easy. He can be trusted with our everything.

If God sees, and we are created in His image, then it follows that we are created to see as He sees. He sees everything from a most holy perspective, and we are called to do the same. It could be said that holiness is the way we see things. Consider what the following verses reveal about holiness and its effect on perspective:

Titus 1:15 – *"To the pure all things are pure"*.

Matthew 5:8 - *"Blessed are the pure in heart for they shall see God."*

Psalm 24:3-4 – *"Who can ascend to the hill of the Lord? Or who can stand in His holy place? He who have clean hands and a pure heart."*

<u>We must see and believe that we are righteous and holy before God.</u>

We can no longer believe who the world tells us we are, nor can we judge ourselves according to our past mistakes and sins. Remember, those things are under the powerful blood of Jesus if we have been born again. His word is truth, and therefore, what He says about us is truth! The old is gone and the new has come! 2 Corinthians 5:17 says, *"Therefore, if anyone is in Christ, he is a new creation; old things have passed away; behold, all things have become new."*

Our hearts have been made pure by the Lord Jesus, and we are being sanctified by the Holy Spirit daily. This means we are already pure, holy, and righteous before the Lord because we have been born again, but as we 'work out our salvation,' the Holy Spirit continues to give us revelation of who we really are. This is the process of revelation, the unveiling, the revealing of truth to our inner man so that when we *"see Him, we will be like Him"* (1 John 3:2).

<u>There is One Spirit—One Stream</u>

Many in our world today would like us to believe

that there are "many roads to God." We know this is not true because Jesus said of Himself in John 14:6, *"I am the way, the truth and the life. No one comes to the Father except through Me."* There is only one road to God and that is through Jesus Christ.

In the same way, once we are born again, there are some who would like for us to believe that scripture is subject to personal interpretation or preference. Some believe that it is okay to pick and choose which parts of the Bible to apply and obey. Now, the Bible is living and active, and as we journey with the Lord, we may read one scripture at a particular point in our journey and it speaks to us one way. At a later time in the journey, we may read that same scripture and it speaks to us in a fresh and new way. However, there is never an exemption for us not to believe ALL of the Bible in its entirety. It is not ok to believe some passages but reject the others. It is equally erroneous to discount a certain part of scripture but hold fast to the rest. Holy Spirit is never confused. There are not 'many streams' or many ways to believe things in the Body of Christ. There is but one true stream.

It is important to remember that each of us in on a personal journey within this stream on our journey of love. We are all at different places. New revelation of scripture comes all along the way. God reveals His precious love to us all along the way. Some believers have just stepped into the stream while others have been on the journey for a long time. Some only have had a few experiences and encounters with the Spirit of Holiness while others have had many. Being at different places within the one stream is a much different concept than there being "many streams". The concept of many streams is one that says we can all believe (or not believe) pieces of the Word and it still be okay.

Ephesians 4:3-6 says, "*Endeavoring to keep the unity of the Spirit in the bond of peace. There is one body and one Spirit, just as you were called in one hope of your calling; one Lord, one faith, one baptism; one God and Father of all, who is above all, and through all, and in you all.*"

This passage makes it very clear that, while we are all on a different leg in this journey of love, we are all being drawn into one beautiful body, to work together under the leadership of the Great Spirit of Holiness. We are to endeavor to become one in the unity of the Spirit. Holy Spirit doesn't waver. As we read in John 16:13, Holy Spirit will not speak on His own authority, but He only speaks what He hears from the Father! God will never tell anyone it is okay to not fully lay hold of His entire Word.

How can it possibly be that people from all walks of life, from all nations and tribes, and from all the doctrines and interpretations of scripture can come together in one accord in the unity of the Spirit? It does not come from believers just agreeing to disagree with each other. Nor does it come by dividing the Word of God up into 'negotiables' and 'non-negotiables'. For example, there is a somewhat common teaching that says that the virgin birth, life, death, burial and resurrection of Jesus Christ are the only non-negotiables and that everything else is negotiable. Nothing could be further from the truth. There is not one word written in scripture that is negotiable. There is no place for our opinion with any word of God.

So the question remains: how can so many people, tribes and tongues come together in the unity of the Spirit? This will only happen if each of us listens to what the Holy Spirit is telling us. He will not tell you one thing and tell another something totally different. He will never contradict Himself, and He is not confused. What Holy Spirit speaks comes straight from the heart and mouth of God.

We have a great assurance of this in John 16:13-14, when Jesus makes His disciples this promise: *"However, when He, the Spirit of truth, has come, He will guide you into all truth; for He will not speak on His own authority, but whatever He hears He will speak; and He will tell you things to come. He will glorify Me, for He will take of what is Mine and declare it to you."* Holy Spirit, the Spirit of Holiness, speaks only what He hears the Father say.

Drawing on this truth, the Bible offers us a visual representation of the journey of holiness. Isaiah 35:8 speaks of a highway of holiness: *"A highway shall be there, and a road and it shall be called a highway to Holiness..."* Every believer is on this highway, having fully submitted to the Lordship and authority of Jesus Christ. The Holy Spirit leads us along this highway to sanctify us and bring us to full maturity, thus transforming us to be that pure and spotless bride prepared for Jesus, our Bridegroom King.

<u>Without Holiness We Cannot See Others as God</u>

Sees Them.

Did you know that how we see God affects how we see others? We have established that God is a holy God, but until there is an understanding of the word "holy," we still fall short of seeing God as He really is.

We can typically fall to one of two extremes in our perception of God. One extreme is when we see God as a sweet, old grandfather that just wants to give us everything we want at the exact time we want it. That sweet grandfather could never discipline us or tell us no. After all, God is love, right?

Quite contrary to this immature view, God is not a genie in a bottle, sitting on the throne just waiting all day to grant our every whim and wish while we go about living life as we please. Without a doubt, God is love just as the Bible says, but in that love and because He is holy, He disciplines us. He actually loves us too much to let us continue to live the way we want to live. We are called to crucify our flesh and be holy as He is holy. Therefore, the perception of God as "wish-granter-in-Chief" falls far short of the truth.

The other extreme is seeing God as a strict disciplinarian waiting for us to mess up so that He can issue a harsh punishment. For many, this is where the biggest misconception of holiness lies. This view leads to the understanding that God is holy and that we are called to be holy, too. According to this perspective, the minute we fall God is furious at us, and we are in big trouble. This misconception of holiness completely leaves out the love of God for His children.

The following two verses will help bring clarity. In the New Living Translation, Hebrews 12:6-9 says,

"6 For the Lord disciplines those He loves, and He punishes each one he accepts as His child. 7 As you endure this divine discipline, remember that God is treating you as His own children. Who ever heard of a child who I s never disciplined by its father? 8 If God doesn't discipline you as he does all of his children it means that you are illegitimate and are not really His children at all. 9 Since we respected our earthly fathers who disciplined us, shouldn't we submit even more the discipline of the Father of our spirits, and live forever?"

This passage gives us a very good picture of both the goodness and the severity of God as He fathers us. Matthew 7:9-11 brings more clarity as well:

"9...what man is there among you who, if his son asks for bread, will give him a stone? 10 Or if he asks for a fish, will he give him a serpent? 11 If you then, being evil, know how to give good gifts to your children, how much more will your Father who is in heaven give good things to those who ask Him!"

The way we see God often stems from the way we see our earthly fathers. We all come from many different walks of life, but we all have this in common: we all have fathers, and they were all human. None of our earthly fathers were perfect. Some were born into a family where the father was absent, and maybe they never even knew their fathers. Others had fathers who were very harsh or strict and who didn't outwardly exhibit love to their children. There are those who had fathers that showed love to their children only when they accomplished a great task or won the trophy, while others had dads that praised them for everything and never brought any sort of discipline when rebellion arose. All of these scenarios and many more make up what we observe in family dynamics.

Now, let's consider how each of these scenarios can affect a person's view of God.

If you are one that had an absentee father, then it is easy to see God as absent - like He's never around when you need Him. You just have to tough it up and go it alone in the world because Daddy's not there to guide you through.

If your father was very harsh and strict, not exhibiting love or affection, then your view of your Heavenly Father is much the same. If this was your experience, you tend to see only the discipline of God and never the love and affection He has for you.

Perhaps your father pushed you in a particular sport, or in getting good grades, or being a part of a certain club or organization. When the report card was all A's, or the trophy was won, he poured out his praise to you, but not so much when the grades were lower, or your game was a little off. This teaches us to believe that we are loved when we perform well. When this happens with our Heavenly Father, we are always striving to perform to win His love.

Some fathers just want to love their kids and make life so easy for them that they never have to encounter disappointment or hardship. Every wish is granted even before they ask. Believe it or not, this can be just as deceiving and dangerous as the other examples because God is not here to be at our beck and call. God requires our obedience, and when we've never been made to obey because there are no rules, we don't have a correct perception of God.

We could go on and on with examples like these, but we can gain an understanding from the ones we've mentioned. Once we realize how much we have projected our view of our earthly fathers on to our Heavenly Father, then we can begin the process of allowing Holy Spirit to bring truth to those areas, removing what doesn't belong and bringing revelation of what does.

What does all of this have to do with the idea that "without holiness we cannot see others as God sees them?" Every relationship we are a part of is affected by how we see God. When we see God as He is, then we will begin to see ourselves as God sees us.

When we see God as a God who only loves us when we win, we see ourselves as failures when we fall, thus believing God is not pleased with us. If that is our mindset, we will project that same unrealistic expectation onto those we are in contact with. We will see them as only useful if they can perform to our expectations. On the other hand, having this image of God can lead to our continually trying to perform to win others' acceptance. That is referred to as people pleasing, and we want none of that. We are called to please God and God alone. We cannot allow fear of not pleasing man to stop us from pleasing God.

When we see God as nothing but a disciplinarian, we tend to think He takes much delight in punishment, so we see ourselves again as not being able to measure up. We walk on eggshells around God, afraid to approach Him. This fear can severely damage our relationships with others.

There are many examples of how our perception of God affects our relationship with others. So how do we break free from these damaging mindsets? Ask Holy Spirit to show you, first of all, how you see the Father. Allow the Spirit of Holiness to meet you in that place to clean you up and heal your heart. Then ask Him to reveal how this has affected your relationship with those around you. He is just waiting for the invitation to come in and start to work!

God extends great grace towards us. That grace is extended to us even when we are being disciplined and chastened. That same grace is available to us to extend to those we come in contact with. Even when an issue must be confronted or a hard truth must be brought to someone we are in relationship with, grace can (and must) abound. When we see God as the gracious Father that He is, we can be gracious to others, as well.

A relevant passage that sums this all up is found in Mark 12:29-31: Jesus answered him, *"The first of all the commandments is: 'Hear, O Israel, the LORD our God, the LORD is one. And you shall love the Lord your God with all your heart, with all your soul, with all your mind, and with all your strength.' This is the first commandment. And the second, like it, is this: 'You shall love your neighbor as yourself'. There is no other commandment greater than these."*

We cannot love our neighbor if we do not love ourselves. Until we receive the love the Father has for us, we are completely unable to love ourselves, thus falling short of loving our neighbor. If Jesus said this is the greatest commandment, shouldn't we go before the Father in all humility and submission and ask Him to do His sanctifying work in our hearts? The Spirit of Holiness will move on our behalf to bring us into a wholeness and a brand new ability to see as God sees, which empowers us to love as God loves!

Walk Holy

In Colossians 2:6, we are commanded to walk holy: *"As you therefore have received Christ Jesus the Lord, so walk in Him."* We received the Lord Jesus by grace through faith (Ephesians 2:8), and that is how we walk out the rest of our journey with the Lord. Because of His grace and mercy towards us, we are made holy, and it is by our faith in Him that we walk out each step and follow each directive that comes from the Spirit of Holiness.

Remember, holiness is apartness. We are set apart for the Lord when we become born again. The Spirit of Holiness is doing His sanctifying work in us, so there must be no agreement with darkness. Let's look at Paul's instructions to the Corinthian church in 2 Corinthians 6:11-7:1:

"11 O Corinthians! We have spoken openly to you, our heart is wide open. 12 You are not restricted by us, but you are restricted by your own affections. 13 Now in return for the same (I speak as to children), you also be open.

14 Do not be unequally yoked together with unbelievers. For what fellowship has righteousness with lawlessness? And what communion has light with darkness? 15 And what accord has Christ with Belial? Or what part has a believer with an unbeliever? 16 And what agreement has the temple of God with idols? For you are the temple of the living God. As God has said:

*"I will dwell in them
And walk among them.
I will be their God,
And they shall be My people."*

17 Therefore

*"Come out from among them
And be separate, says the Lord.
Do not touch what is unclean,
And I will receive you."
18 "I will be a Father to you,
And you shall be My sons and daughters,
Says the Lord Almighty."*

7:1 Therefore, having these promises, beloved, let us cleanse ourselves from all filthiness of the flesh and spirit, perfecting holiness in the fear of God."

The apostle Paul commands the church to be set apart, to be different from those who are not a part of the Body of Christ. We are to be salt and light to the rest of the world. In Matthew 5:13-16 Jesus tells those at the Sermon on the Mount,

"13 You are the salt of the earth; but if the salt loses its flavor, how shall it be seasoned? It is then good for nothing but to be thrown out and trampled underfoot by men.

14 You are the light of the world. A city that is set on a hill cannot be hidden. 15 Nor do they light a lamp and put it under a basket, but on a lampstand, and it gives light to all who are in the house. 16 Let your light so shine before men, that they may see your good works and glorify your Father in heaven."

We are set apart to glorify our Father in heaven. We are made in His image and likeness, and we have His very Spirit living in us. We are to model and exemplify His very Spirit to all that we come in contact with. We are to be holy and walk as He walked so that others may come to know Him through our good works.

1 John 2:15-17
"15 Do not love the word or the things in the world. If anyone loves the world the love of the Father is not in him. 16 For all that is in the world—the lust of the flesh, the lust of the eyes, and the pride of life—is not of the Father but is of the world. 17 And the world is passing away, and the lust of it; but he who does the will of God abides forever."

By just these few passages it is clear that we are to reflect Jesus in all that we do, and in order to do that, we must put away all that is not of Him.

Hindrances to Holiness

In addition to our surrender to the Spirit of Holiness, it is imperative to know that we also have an enemy whose sole purpose is to keep us from the love of our Father. In doing so, our enemy keeps us from walking in the holiness of the Lord. In John 10:10, Jesus tells us that "*the thief does not come except to kill, steal and destroy. I have come that they might have life, and that they may have it more abundantly.*" The thief, satan, and his demonic forces, began their work with mankind in the Garden of Eden, and they haven't stopped trying to hinder the glory ever since.

Sometimes the problem is just that our "Grade A Flesh" gets in the way and hinders us from the call and destiny of holiness in our lives. Let's look at a few of the most common hindrances to living in holiness.

Judgments: Judgments are ungodly perceptions or expectations. They can include judging others or judging ourselves. As we learned earlier, for example, when we see God as an unkind, harsh, and impatient God, we tend to act that way toward ourselves and others. We expect nothing but perfection and become terribly intolerant when we see anything less. Remember, we are called to see as God sees, and how we see God affects how we see ourselves and others.

I am reminded of a childhood memory that

could illustrate what this might look like. When my brother and I were very young, our mother shopped weekly at a little "dime store." My brother and I had so much fun trying on the colored sunshades in that store. These shades had all sorts of lenses. Some were red, some were green. There were yellow, blue, purple, orange, and every color in between. We thought it was so funny to put these on because, of course, they made everything we looked at appear that color. The people would be purple if we were wearing the purple shades. They would be orange if that was the color of the shades we wore.

As believers in Jesus, we can put on "shades of judgment." These shades tend to come from our past mistakes, from being offended, or from being hurt and wounded in some way. Instead of the colored lenses, we can put on "shades" of jealousy or anger. Perhaps you saw jealousy rear its ugly head in a person, and immediately you put on those shades of jealousy. Now all you can see when you see that person is jealousy because you haven't removed the shades.

There are shades that see only inconsideration in a person. Maybe someone was very inconsiderate at some point with you, and you picked up those shades of inconsideration. Now, inconsideration is all you see in them. It doesn't matter if that person brings you flowers every day. As long as you wear the shades of inconsideration, you will always see them as inconsiderate. We could go on and on.

Not only do we view others through these colored and distorted lenses, but we can also view ourselves through these many kinds of shades. These shades tend to be tinted from past mistakes as well. The Spirit of Holiness is asking us to allow Him to remove these shades of judgment from us because they are hindering us from walking as Jesus walked. Removing these shades will most certainly involve forgiving both others and ourselves. We must forgive the offense (or perceived offense) that caused us to put on the shades in the first place.

Another step that Holy Spirit will lead us in is to release all the pain that came from that offense. We release the pain by surrendering it to Him. Many people are ineffective in working through offense because they are not honest with themselves or with God. They may not realize that they're holding on to something, or they may not want to "tell on" someone. Nevertheless, releasing offense is only effective if we tell the truth about what happened and its effects on us. In other words, we must tell our Father exactly what happened and how it made us feel. When that friend lashed out in anger, it hurt! When the co-worker spoke something that embarrassed you in front of others, it hurt! However, when we acknowledge the pain, choose to forgive, and release that pain to God, we begin to experience not only freedom from judgment, but deep healing as well. Moreover, as we go through these two steps of forgiveness and letting go of the hurt, the Father exchanges those hurts for His goodness.

The Spirit of Holiness will lead you perfectly to set you free from all judgments. We must realize though, that taking off these shades of judgment is not a one-time event. Offenses and hurts will continue to come our way. As we grow, we will learn to recognize them for what they are and choose not to pick them up and put them on as often as we once did. However, there will still be times when those shades are over our eyes before we know it. Holy Spirit, in His goodness, will show us they are there, and we simply go back to the Father, repent, forgive, and release. He is good, and He loves to see His children run to Him in repentance!

Traditions of man: Traditions of man refer to the ways people try to replace true obedience to God with manmade rules or ideas. The traditions of man create a huge barrier in the area of hindrances to holiness. This stems from an incorrect view of what holiness really is and from trying to become holy through our own power and works of the flesh. Even though, as believers, our spirit man is holy because He resides there, we know our soul is a work in progress. Many times we try to make ourselves holy in our own strength, and that will never work. Let's take a look at a few of these traditions of man.

Fasting and prayer are both very important parts of our journey with the Lord. However, they can be turned into very legalistic activities. Even prayer, when carried out from a heart of legalism or self-righteousness, becomes a barrier to true communion with the Holy Spirit. Matthew 6:5-7 says, *"And when you pray, you shall not be like the hypocrites. For they love to pray standing in the synagogues and on the corners of the streets, that they may be seen by men. Assuredly, I say to you, they have their reward. But you, when you pray, go into your room, and when you have shut your door, pray to your Father who is in the secret place; and your Father who sees in secret will reward you openly. And when you pray, do not use vain repetitions as the heathen do. For they think that they will be heard for their many words."*

Prayer is a special, truly beautiful gift given to us to communicate with our Heavenly Father. Nevertheless, this gift can be easily twisted into something religious and regimented, done for show before men to make us look pious and holy. As Jesus discussed in the verses above, that kind of prayer does not move the Father's heart.

Fasting is also a very important facet of our journey, but it too can become a religious exercise. Jesus addresses this issue in Matthew 6:16-18: *"Moreover, when you fast, do not be like the hypocrites, with a sad countenance. For they disfigure their faces that they may appear to men to be fasting. Assuredly, I say to you, they have their reward. But you, when you fast, anoint your head and wash your face, so that you do not appear to men to be fasting, but to your Father who is in the secret place; and your Father who sees in secret will reward you openly."*

We can see by these two passages that holiness isn't an outward act to be viewed by man. True holiness comes from the Spirit of Holiness working in, with, and through us from the inside out. If you will notice in both of the previous scriptures, their prayer and fasting were done in public so that others could see their acts, and yet, the Father is in the secret place. That is the place that really matters!

Another tradition of man that is errantly used to portray holiness is the way we dress or the way we wear our hair. There are religious traditions out there that teach that a woman must only wear dresses and never cut her hair. There are debates about cosmetics and jewelry, as well. Whatever your choice of dress is, remember that how you dress doesn't make you holy. We want to always dress in ways that honor and glorify God, but again, holiness isn't an outward appearance. Holiness begins on the inside. It is not a work of the flesh.

In addition to appearances and apparel, diet is also a hot topic today, but it is really nothing new. Clean and unclean foods are mentioned all throughout the Bible. In the Old Testament, God made a list of clean and unclean foods for His people as they journeyed through life. These restrictions were given to them predominantly because the unclean foods were unhealthy to the body and would cause His people sickness and even death if they were eaten.

In the New Testament, clean and unclean foods remained an issue but had become more of a tradition of man and a religious act. In Acts 10:9-16, Peter was actually corrected by God regarding clean and unclean foods: *"The next day, as they went on their journey and drew near the city, Peter went up on the housetop to pray about the sixth hour. Then he became very hungry and wanted to eat; but while they made ready, he fell into a trance and saw heaven opened and an object like a great sheet bound at the four corners, descending to him and let down to the earth. In it were all kinds of four-footed animals of the earth, wild beasts, creeping things, and birds of the air. And a voice came to him, "Rise, Peter; kill and eat." But Peter said, "Not so, Lord! For I have never eaten anything common or unclean."*

And a voice spoke to him again the second time, 'What God has cleansed you must not call common.' This was done three times. And the object was taken up into heaven again."

What had begun in the Old Testament as guidelines for health and safety, had, in the New Testament, become religious - a sign of holiness according to the traditions of man. God used Peter's vision to release truth about what really made someone holy. We understand that this is not a license to be gluttonous. We are told in 1 Corinthians 6:19 that our bodies are the temple of the Holy Spirit, and we want to nourish and feed our bodies correctly in order to be healthy and to carry out the mandate given to us by the Lord. We do not want to be careless and neglectful in the way we eat, but it is not a sign of holiness.

Continuing this exploration of traditions of man, church attendance has become a modern-day measuring stick for holiness. Hebrews 10:24-25 teaches us, *"And let us consider one another in order to stir up love and good works, not forsaking the assembling of ourselves together, as is the manner of some, but exhorting one another, ad so much the more as you see the Day approaching."*

It is important that we gather together with other believers to be encouraged and to learn. We need each other! However, when church attendance becomes something that "we have to do," or we fear someone driving by the church on Sunday morning and not seeing our car there, we've missed the point.

When I (Danetta) was a little girl in Sunday School, it was a common thing for our teachers to have a board on the wall. The board would have a list of tasks and a square to put a gold star in if the items on that list were accomplished that morning. For example, some of the questions on that board were the following: 1) Did you memorize your verse for the week? 2) Are you staying for church today? 3) Did you bring an offering? 4) Did you read your Bible every day? 5) Did you study your Sunday School lesson?

Now, none of these questions are bad, and the intention of the teacher was to emphasize the importance of the items on the list. I was blessed to be raised in a home where my parents helped me with these essential parts of a Christian walk. They made sure I was staying for church and that I had memorized my verse because they instilled in us the importance of God's word. They made sure we had an offering because they were teaching us to give and tithe. Getting the gold stars was easy for me because I had help.

However, I began to notice that some of my little friends didn't get as many gold stars on their charts. Several didn't even have a Bible at home to read from, much less memorize verses. Most didn't have a parent that brought them to church. Some even had to ride their bikes to church, and having money for an offering wasn't an option for them. They left Sunday School feeling defeated and embarrassed because they didn't measure up. If they could have articulated their feelings as a little child, I'm sure they would say they felt "unholy"...not good enough. Yet, they sacrificed much more to be at church that day than I did. Holiness cannot be reduced to gold stars on a poster board.

Much like the prayer and fasting on the street corner, these charts and gold stars became a point of pride for kids like me. They were a place of humiliation and heartache for those little ones who didn't have access to such things. Did my getting the gold stars each week and going to church make me any more holy? Absolutely not! Unfortunately, many times it just made me boastful and proud. A well-known teacher in the body of Christ said something that has stuck with me for many years. She said, "Going to church doesn't make you a Christian any more than sitting in a garage makes you a car!" It's all about the heart, and the heart is where holiness begins.

Yet another tradition of man, materialism can be a hindrance to holiness. There are false teachings out there that would have us believe if we aren't wealthy, we aren't blessed. These teachings hold that our financial status and what we own are a sign of blessing and holiness. Truth be told, God wants to bless His children and scripture tells us that He does precisely that, but it isn't necessarily a sign of holiness.

On the other hand, having wealth can also be viewed as being unholy in some of the traditional teachings of man. That philosophy teaches that being a pauper is a sign of holiness. Neither side is accurate because materialism isn't a standard by which to measure holiness.

Not only does materialism lead to a warped view, but even our very works and actions can be manipulated to imply a fake sense of holiness when measured by the traditions of man. The bottom line is that we can do good works all day long, but if we do them to be seen by man for attention, or to make ourselves feel good, then we have our reward. Contrary to the views of the world, our Father looks at the heart. He does not judge on the outward appearance of man, and He is far more concerned with our spiritual condition than our physical circumstances.

Unbelief: Unbelief requires little explanation. It simply means that we don't believe God or His Word. Our unbelief is a hindrance to holiness. In order to please the Lord, we must have faith. From the very beginning of our walk with God, faith (believing) has been foundational. In order to become born again, we had to believe that Jesus was born of a virgin, lived a sinless life, died on the cross, and rose again to purchase us by paying for our sins. Every step of our journey since that moment has required us to believe what He says and to follow Him.

We must believe who God says we are. We must believe that He desires to give us good things. We must believe that He has sent the great Spirit of Holiness to partner with us to see us healed and delivered. We must believe that He will complete the work He began in us, and in believing, we must submit to the Spirit completely. There is no room for unbelief because it will always hinder holiness.

It is imperative for us to understand that holiness is an inward work of Holy Spirit. It is not something we can accomplish on our own by any of these actions or attitudes we have discussed. We can appear to be so holy and righteous outwardly and still be a mess on the inside. The appearance of holiness on the outside is nothing but a façade. As believers, we should yearn for the Spirit of Holiness to do His work deep in our hearts by shining His light on all that is unholy. We should desire more than anything for those unholy areas to be removed so that the very character of God can grow and shine in us. We want to be the real deal when it comes to holiness, and the real deal is the Spirit of Holiness doing the work in us.

Ask Holy Spirit to begin to show you those masks and facades you've put on, and allow Him to begin to clean house in the very depths of your soul. He is ready to move on your behalf, making you holy as He is holy.

See God in Your Circumstances

We discussed earlier in this book that one of God's names is El Roi (God sees). We've also learned that holiness is seeing as God sees, and until we see God as He truly is, we cannot see others as He sees them.

There is one more aspect of "seeing" that should be discussed, and that is seeing God in our circumstances. We have a promise from God in Hebrews 13:5-6, "*...For He Himself has said, 'I will never leave you nor forsake you.' So we may boldly say: 'The Lord is my helper; I will not fear. What* *can man do to me?'"*

If we've lived very long on this earth, we know that life isn't always easy or fun. There are things that happen in life that present challenges and heartaches, and yet, God has promised us that He will be with us in the midst of it all. The question becomes, "Do we see Him in those circumstances?" When we are going through those difficult seasons, it is very important to look for Him.

He is with us in every trial. He is with us in every battle we fight. We never go through these times alone, but we must believe that He is there. We must believe that He is for us and not against us, and we must believe that we always have the victory because He, the Victorious One, has never left our side.

When persecutions come our way - and they will - He is there. He is strengthening us for the battle. He has given His angels charge over us, according to Psalm 91. When our hearts are broken and we are battle weary, He is there to be strong in every place that we are weak.

When delays come our way and it seems like the mountain in front of us won't move, He is in the waiting room with us. When we've prayed and prayed and haven't seen the breakthrough we are desperate for, He is still there. He is long-suffering. He stays!

When our relationships are less than what we expected and people hurt us, He is there to mend our broken hearts. When we are struggling with a spouse, or grieving over a loved one or crying out over a prodigal child, He is there to hold us and comfort us. He is there to reassure us that we will be okay.

As we learn to see God in our circumstances, we must ask, "What is God doing in this situation? What is He making me to be?" In this life we will face trials. We will face many battles on a variety battlefields. There will be spiritual battles. There will be emotional, physical, and mental battles, as well.

We will all, believers and unbelievers, face persecutions in this life. For those who are believers, we must remember what Jesus said in John 15:18-19, *"If the world hates you, you know that it hated Me before it hated you. If you were of the world, the world would love its own. Yet because you are not of the world, but I chose you out of the world, therefore the world hates you."*

We will face delays and what may seem to be unanswered prayers. There will always be relationship issues we must deal with. So again, we must continually seek what God is doing during these times. How is He using the circumstances in my life to make me in to the person He created me to be? As His children, we are referred to in His Word as "clay in the Potter's hand." We are being molded and shaped into the image and likeness of our Father. God uses these circumstances that come our way as times of shaping, pruning and refining. He is making us to be *PURE GOLD*.

Psalm 27:1-6
"1 The Lord is my light and salvation; whom shall I fear? The Lord is the strength of my life;

> *of whom shall I be afraid? 2 When the wicked came against me to eat up my flesh, my enemies and foes stumbled and fell. 3 Though an army may encamp against me, my heart shall not fear; though war may rise against me, in this I will be confident. 4 One thing I have desired of the Lord, that will I seek: That I may dwell in the house of the Lord all the days of my life. To behold the beauty of the Lord and to inquire in His temple, 5 for in the time of trouble He shall hide me in His pavilion; in the secret place of His tabernacle He shall hide me; He shall set me upon a rock. 6 And now my head shall be lifted up above my enemies all around me; therefore I will offer sacrifices of joy in His tabernacle; I will sing, yes, I will sing praises to the Lord."*

This is a powerful text reflecting David's heart while in the midst of trials. It is very apparent in this passage that David's heart remained close to the Father's heart. While his circumstances caused him to be pressed and surrounded, he saw God in those circumstances. He felt confident that His God would cause him to prevail over his enemies and he remained true to one thing: to dwell with His God!

We can also glean much about seeing God in our circumstances from the Apostle Paul's letter to the church in Philippi. As the letter says, Paul and Timothy had suffered loss and persecution along their journeys, but Paul still wrote, *"But what things were gain to me, these I have counted loss for Christ. Yet indeed I also count all things loss for the excellence of the knowledge of Christ Jesus my Lord, for whom I have suffered the loss of all things, and count them rubbish, that I may gain Christ and be found in Him, not having a righteousness of my own, which is from the law, but that which is through faith in Christ, the righteousness which is from God by faith; that I may know Him and the power of His resurrection, and the fellowship of His sufferings, being conformed to His death, if, by any means, I may attain to the resurrection from the dead...Not that I have attained it or am already perfected; but I press on, that I may lay hold of that for which Christ Jesus has also laid hold of me. Brethren, I do not count myself to have apprehended; but one thing I do, forgetting those things which are behind and reaching forward to those things which are ahead. I press toward the goal for the prize of the upward call of God in Christ Jesus*" (Philippians 3:7-14).

Notice that in both of these scriptures the writers refer to "*one thing.*" God's holy presence is our "one thing." In our everyday lives, through good times and bad, we are to abide in Him, clinging to and looking for His presence in each delay, in each trial, in each persecution and in each joyous occasion. Through it all we persevere, knowing '*that all things work together for good to those who love God, to those who are the called according to His purpose*' (Romans 8:28).

The Lord Tests the Hearts and Minds of Men and Women

As we have seen, there will be tests along the way in our journeys. There are times that God is actually the one doing the testing of the hearts and minds of mankind. One definition from the Strong's Concordance for the word test is 'to examine, prove, scrutinize, try (of gold, persons, the heart, man of God to be tried, proved)." God is not testing us to be cruel or because He is angry with us. We are tested so that we can see the areas we fall short in. The Spirit of Holiness comes in to aid us in correcting and repenting of these areas so that they can be pruned away. This pruning allows for great growth and refining.

Psalm 11:5: *"The Lord tests the righteous..."*.

2 Corinthians 13:5-6: *"Examine yourselves as to whether you are in the faith. Test yourselves. Do you not know yourselves, that Jesus Christ is in you? —unless indeed you are disqualified."*

2 Corinthians 2:9: *"For to this end I also wrote, that I might put you to the test, whether you are obedient in all things."*

Proverbs 17:3: *"The refining pot is for silver and the furnace for gold, but the Lord tests the hearts."*

Scripture makes it clear that God does, indeed, test the hearts of man. Through this testing, we become aware of the specific areas of our lives where our weaknesses and shortcomings lie. It makes clear our areas of disobedience and rebellion. Once these are made known to us, we can run to the Father in repentance, fully receiving His forgiveness and restoration, allowing Holy Spirit to sanctify us in those places.

The late Kim Clement, a Prophet to the Nations, taught of 15 tests that we will receive with every revelation.

1. The Time Test – Wait it Out

Many times in our journey with the Lord, we are called to wait. It can be hard! Our faith is tested in the wait, and yet, learning to wait *in faith* is an area of growth that most of us still need to be perfected in. Abraham and Sarah received the promise of a son, but they waited twenty-five years for the fulfillment of that promise. Yet, they waited and they held fast to the Word of the Lord over their lives, and the Bible says it was counted to them as righteousness. The Spirit of Holiness often uses a waiting to work in us to make us more like our God, who is long-suffering. Patience, long-suffering, is actually a part of the fruit of Holy Spirit that dwells in us. The 'time test' will refine us to be more like Him.

2. The Word Test

The word inside of you will be tested in so many ways. The original test in Genesis came in the form of the serpent (satan) asking Eve, "Did God really say?" The enemy has not changed his tactics. If he can get us to doubt the word and what God has spoken, he has upended our faith. We must grow to be a people that declares in full faith, "God said it and I believe it!"

3. The Character Test

The fruit of the Spirit is found in Galatians 5:22-23: *"But the fruit of the Spirit is love, joy, peace, longsuffering kindness, goodness, faithfulness, gentleness, self-control."* The fruit of the Spirit grows in our lives making us more mature as we go along day to day. There will often be character tests along the way. No doubt we could all look at these nine facets of the fruit of the Spirit and see places where we haven't been perfected yet. Character tests will arise for us so that we can grow in each of these areas. Every born-again believer has an anointing from the Holy One. The Character Test causes our character to line up with God's anointing on our lives.

4. The Motivation Test

What is my motive in doing what I do? While men may look at outward appearances, God always looks at the motive of the heart. Matthew 6:5-6 tells us, *"And when you pray, you shall not be like the hypocrites. For they love to pray standing in the synagogues and on the corners of the streets, that they may be seen by men. Assuredly, I say to you, they have their reward. But you, when you pray, go into your room, and when you have shut your door, pray to your Father who is in the secret place; and your Father who sees in secret will reward you openly."*

Jesus goes on to teach us in Matthew 6:16-18, *"Moreover, when you fast, do not be like the hypocrites, with a sad countenance. For they disfigure their faces that they may appear to men to be fasting. Assuredly, I say to you, they have their reward. But you, when you fast, anoint your head and wash your face so that you do not appear to men to be fasting but to your Father who is in the secret place; and you Father who sees in secret will reward you openly."*

The only way we can remain motivated during the testing times is to remain focused on the Lord.

When our focus is on man, what man thinks of us, and worldly things, we will not stay motivated to do the works we are called to do; but when we keep our eyes on the One in the secret place, we will know who we are. We will know what we are called to do, and we will not be double minded. We will be like David when he was in the cave hiding from Saul and said, "*My heart is fixed, oh God. I will sing praise.*" (Psalm 57:7)

5. The Servant Test

Jesus modeled servanthood to us beautifully as He walked the earth. One of the most astounding examples of servanthood is when He washed His disciples' feet only hours before going to the cross, even knowing that they all would soon betray Him. This account is found in John 13, but let's focus on verses 12-15. "*So when He had washed their feet, taken His garments, and sat down again He said to them, 'Do you know what I have done to you? You all Me Teacher and Lord, and you say well for so I am. If I then, your Lord and Teacher, have washed your feet, you also ought to wash another's feet. For I have given you an example, that you should do as I have done to you.'*"

Pride will always tell us, "I don't want to serve anymore." The best way to keep ourselves in check is to serve.

6. The Wilderness Test

The wilderness is a picture of a dry and lonely place. Many times is our journeys with the Lord, we can feel like nothing is going our way, as if the prayers we have prayed will never be answered, or the things we have longed for will never come to pass. It can be a place where we have been for a while, knowing in all confidence that God has spoken a word to us and we've yet to see it come to pass.

It is very easy to give up hope during the times in the wilderness, but these can actually be incredible times. God still provides for us in these wilderness times. He is faithful!

7. The Misunderstanding Test

None of us enjoy being misunderstood. Our first natural response to being misunderstood is to lash out, fight back and work to prove to others who we are or what it is we are trying to say.

Jesus was without a doubt the most misunderstood person that has ever lived. It is written of Jesus in Acts 8:32-33, *"He was led like a sheep to the slaughter. And as a lamb is silent before the shearers, He did not open His mouth. He was humiliated and received no justice."* (NLT)

Jesus, the very Son of God, was thought to be a heretic and a liar by many. Even in this, He did not fight back when men criticized Him and tried to discredit Him. He knew that His Father would bring strong victory and justice.

Psalm 26 assures us that vindication is from God.

8. The Patience Test

I'm sure we can agree that waiting is no easy thing to do. We all tend to want what we want...and we want it NOW! However, God has a different idea about patience. He uses the waiting times to teach us about patience because we grow and mature through these tests and times. In James 1:2-4 we read, *"My brethren, count it all joy when you fall into various trials, knowing that the testing of your faith produces patience. But let patience have its perfect work, that you may be perfect and complete, lacking nothing."*

Wait on the Lord. Do not act out of impatience!

9. The Frustration Test

Frustration comes on all of us at one time or another. When we are frustrated, we lose our peace, and everything seems to be closing in on us. During this test, the key is to not worry and to not act out of impatience or discouragement. Remember that we are examples to others and God will vindicate us.

10. The Discouragement Test

Discouragement means "the loss of courage." David was discouraged often in many of the Psalms because he knew the enemy was rising up against him. In Psalm 42:11 we read in the NLT, *"Why am I discouraged? Why is my heart so sad? I will put my hope in God! I will praise Him again—my Savior and my God."* We do not act when we know we are discouraged. Instead, we wait knowing that God will come.

11. The Warfare Test

During the warfare test, we will be met with much

resistance. There are many ways the enemy will come against us, but whatever way it is, know that it is a time of war! We must be very skillful in hearing the voice of God during this test to know how to combat these attacks. We see in Psalm 144:1-2 that there is a time to fight, and a time to take refuge, standing stil in the shelter of the Lord: *"Blessed be the Lord my Rock, who trains my hands for war, and my fingers for battle—My lovingkindness and my fortress, my high tower and my deliverer, my shield and the One in whom I take refuge, who subdues my people under me."*

12. The Self-Will Test

God gave us a will from the very beginning of time. Our self-will says to us, "I'm going to do things my way." As we take up our cross and follow Jesus daily (Luke 9:23), we are dying to that self-will. When we act out of self-will, we are making things all about us, when everything in our lives should be all about God. It is a privilege to walk with God. Stubbornness and self-will should have no place.

13. The Vision Test

In the vision test, we have perceived something from the Lord about the future. We've been given a vision about something to come. We believe what we have seen and are determined to receive the promise. Suddenly, events, people, and worldly things begin to come against that vision. Someone or something may have even acted contrary to it. That leaves an open door for doubt: "Do I really believe in the vision? Did I really see what I thought I saw or hear what I thought I heard?" God is watching to see if we really do believe.

14. The Obedience Test

God checks to see if we will be obedient to Him. To get to the next place with the Lord, we must be obedient now! We will gain momentum into tomorrow as we are obedient to what we've been given to do today. We must be obedient in the smallest of tasks and not take on the attitude of, "That is just too menial for me." Never get too big to do the little things!

15. The Promotion Test

Sometimes opportunities that come to you are NOT an open door from the Lord. No matter how good things seem, if something isn't from the Lord, quickly say "NO" to it. The enemy will act like it is a promotion for you but it is not. Not every opportunity that comes to you will be good for you. Do not be led by the offers of money or fame. When the door opens from the Father, you will know it and promotion will come!

In conclusion, Lance Wallnau teaches about the journey with the Spirit of Holiness like this:

> "Hand...the tips of the fingers are the prophecies over your life and in between the fingers are the ups and downs that no one tells you about in that process of coming into your destiny and fulfilling those prophetic words and promises."

There will certainly be ups and downs, but the late Kim Clement says, "The place of your pain is the place of your reign!" Do not be discouraged because according to 2 Corinthians 2:14, *"Now thanks be to God who always leads us in triumph in Christ, and through us diffuses the fragrance of His knowledge in every place."*

We want to be a holy people, seeing as God sees. When we see as God sees, we see the true prophetic. We see the power of God demonstrated. Our faith arises. Increase, multiplication, and dominion happen both in us and around us, and most importantly of all ... love rules!

We are never on this journey alone. The Spirit of Holiness - THE GREAT HOLY SPIRIT - never leaves us. He never fails us. He never will forsake us. We can rest on the promise that He is completing the beautiful work He began in us through His power, His love and His purpose for us!

Prayer for Salvation

If you have not made Jesus Christ your personal Lord and Savior, and you desire this with all your heart, then please, join me in prayer:

"Heavenly Father, I choose to believe with all my heart, Your love for me. I believe that Jesus Christ is Your Son, the Son of God, and that He is God in the flesh. I believe that You sent Him to this earth to save me. Thank You. I believe He died on the cross for my sins and He was dead and buried three days, and then rose again from the dead and that He ascended to Heaven and is now seated at Your right hand and is returning again.

Father, please forgive me for all my sin and iniquity and I choose to forgive others who have sinned against me. I give You all my heart and choose to live with You forever. I believe I have been born again according to Your Word and that I have been transferred out of the kingdom of darkness and into the kingdom of light. I declare I am forgiven and healed! Now, I ask for Holy Spirit to fill me. Jesus, baptize me in Holy Spirit and fullness in order that I may know You intimately and serve You all my days.

Thank You, Lord, for loving me. Amen."

Scriptures:

John 14:6
"6 Jesus said to him, 'I am the way, the truth, and the life. No one comes to the Father except through Me.'"

Romans 10:8-13
"8 But what does it say? 'The word is near you, in your mouth and in your heart' (that is, the word of faith which we preach): 9 that if you confess with your mouth the Lord Jesus and believe in your heart that God has raised Him from the dead, you will be saved. 10 For with the heart one believes unto righteousness, and with the mouth confession is made unto salvation. 11 For the Scripture says, 'Whoever believes on Him will not be put to shame.' 12 For there is no distinction between Jew and Greek, for the same Lord over all is rich to all who call upon Him. 13 For 'whoever calls on the name of the Lord shall be saved.'"

John 3:3-8, 16-18
"3 Jesus answered and said to him, 'Most assuredly, I say to you, unless one is born again, he cannot see the kingdom of God.' 4 Nicodemus said to Him, 'How can a man be born when he is old? Can he enter a second time into his mother's womb and be born?' 5 Jesus answered, 'Most assuredly, I say to you, unless one is born of water and the Spirit, he cannot enter the kingdom of God. 6 That which is born of the flesh is flesh, and that which is born of the Spirit is spirit. 7 Do not marvel that I said

to you, "You must be born again." 8 The wind blows where it wishes, and you hear the sound of it, but cannot tell where it comes from and where it goes. So is everyone who is born of the Spirit.'"

"16 For God so loved the world that He gave His only begotten Son, that whoever believes in Him should not perish but have everlasting life. 17 For God did not send His Son into the world to condemn the world, but that the world through Him might be saved. 18 'He who believes in Him is not condemned; but he who does not believe is condemned already, because he has not believed in the name of the only begotten Son of God.'"

II Corinthians 5:17
"17 Therefore, if anyone is in Christ, he is a new creation; old things have passed away; behold, all things have become new."

I Corinthians 15:3-5
"3 For I delivered to you first of all that which I also received: that Christ died for our sins according to the Scriptures, 4 and that He was buried, and that He rose again the third day according to the Scriptures, 5 and that He was seen by Cephas, then by the twelve."

II Corinthians 5:21
"21 For He made Him who knew no sin to be sin for us, that we might become the righteousness of God in Him."

Colossians 1:13-14
"13 He has delivered us from the power of dark-

ness and conveyed us into the kingdom of the Son of His love, 14 in whom we have redemption through His blood, the forgiveness of sins."

Luke 11:9-13
"9 So I say to you, ask, and it will be given to you; seek, and you will find; knock, and it will be opened to you. 10 For everyone who asks receives, and he who seeks finds, and to him who knocks it will be opened. 11 If a son asks for bread from any father among you, will he give him a stone? Or if he asks for a fish, will he give him a serpent instead of a fish? 12 Or if he asks for an egg, will he offer him a scorpion? 13 If you then, being evil, know how to give good gifts to your children, how much more will your heavenly Father give the Holy Spirit to those who ask Him!"

Acts 1:8
"8 But you shall receive power when the Holy Spirit has come upon you; and you shall be witnesses to Me in Jerusalem, and in all Judea and Samaria, and to the end of the earth."

I Timothy 3:16
"16 And without controversy great is the mystery of godliness:

God was manifested in the flesh,
Justified in the Spirit,
Seen by angels,
Preached among the Gentiles,
Believed on in the world,
Received up in glory."

Fresh Infilling of Holy Spirit

Acts 1:8
"8 But you shall receive power when the Holy Spirit has come upon you; and you shall be witnesses to Me in Jerusalem, and in all Judea and Samaria, and to the end of the earth."

If you have been born again and filled with Holy Spirit and you desire MORE and want to encounter the Lord's presence afresh and anew, please join me in prayer:

"Father, in the name of Jesus, I thank You for loving me and I ask according to Ephesians 1:17-19, that You would give me the spirit of wisdom and revelation in the knowledge of Him, Jesus, and the eyes of my understanding would be enlightened; that I may know what is the hope of His calling and what are the riches of the glory of His inheritance in the saints, and what is the exceeding greatness of His power toward us who believe, according to the working of His mighty power towards us who believe, according to the working of His mighty power which He worked in Christ when He raised Him from the dead and seated Him at His right hand in the heavenly places. Amen.

Father, according to Colossians 3:9-12, I ask in Jesus name, that I would be filled with the knowledge of His will in all wisdom and spiritual understanding; that I would walk worthy of the Lord, fully pleasing Him, being fruitful in every good work and increasing in the knowledge of God; strengthened with all might, according to His glorious power. Amen.

I surrender and yield my life to the fullness of Holy Spirit; His power and anointing; the spirit of wisdom and revelation; counsel and might; the spirit of the fear of the Lord and knowledge according to Isaiah 11:2, in Jesus' name. Amen."

The Garden Training Center, Inc.
The Apostolic School of Ministry

The Garden Apostolic Training Center is a place that fosters spiritual growth. The center provides training to equip believers in Jesus Christ for the work of the ministry and to be victorious and free in all areas of their lives through the supernatural empowerment of the Holy Spirit. For more information check out **thegardenstc.org**.

The Garden Gathering Church

The purpose of The Garden Gathering Church is to encourage believers in Jesus Christ: to fully embrace the love of God; to walk in freedom; to carry His presence and glory; and to be equipped and trained for the work of the ministry through worship, teachings, and impartation.

> *"It's all about Love. When you see His eyes of Love for you, nothing else matters. That's it. That's all you need to know."*
>
> *-Brandy Helton*

www.ingramcontent.com/pod-product-compliance
Lightning Source LLC
Chambersburg PA
CBHW020547080526
44583CB00013B/1040